11 Things
YOUR
PRODUCER
WANTS YOU TO KNOW

Bridging the Gap Between Music Producers
and the Artists They Produce

GLENN "GK JONES" GILLIARD II

Book Jacket Design Glenn Gilliard II
Cover Photo Credit Terrance Zackery
Interior Book Design by The Author's Mentor
www.theAuthorsMentor.com

ISBN: 978-0-578-77041-3
Also available as an eBook
Published by GK Jones Productions, LLC
www.GKJonesProductions.com

PUBLISHED IN THE UNITED STATES OF AMERICA

This book is dedicated to
David Jones Sr. and Armond V. Brown

"Be your own artist, and always be confident in what you're doing. If you're not going to be confident, you might as well not be doing it."
- Aretha Franklin

AUTHOR'S NOTE

Before you begin reading, this book is solely based on my years of experience and personal interactions in the Music Industry. Nothing is guaranteed in your own interactions and results may vary. I would advise anyone when dealing with contracts to seek legal assistance by way of an attorney. Familiarizing yourself with legal documents is recommended however, when making major decisions it is important to seek legal counsel. Lastly, all music professionals do not do business the same way and by the time you read this book it is possible that industry standard practices may have changed.

TABLE OF CONTENTS

11 Things Your Producer Wants You to Know

"The beautiful thing about learning is that nobody can take it away from you." - BB King

INTRODUCTION

THERE IS A GAP IN THE INDUSTRY BETWEEN MUSIC PRODUCERS and Artists. In many cases Producers are looked at to make a number of compositions, submit them to a middleman and never interact with the Artist themselves. So, in turn, the Artist doesn't know the Producer personally. They only know the composition that they wrote to or liked the most. In other instances, an Artist may have a main Producer they work with and make wonderful music together. The idea here is to get you, "The Artist" to the point where you find your perfect creative match in a Music Producer.

I have witnessed many situations in my earlier years of Production where an Artist's label wouldn't even know how to get in touch with the Music Producer. This happens because truckloads of music get poured into inboxes with no direct connection between the tracks and the music creator. By the time an album is set to come out, the Artist doesn't even know who made the track and the middleman can't even remember where it came from. I am looking to help bridge the gap between creatives to grow healthy working relationships.

We must bridge the gap between the Artist & the Producer...

Some of the greatest records ever made came from a close Producer and Artist relationship when you think about it. Whether you are a seasoned Artist or an up and coming Artist looking to really make an impact, I believe this book will share some much-needed information from a Producer's mind directly to you. Good business relationships will allow creativity to reach levels it may not have in your career thus far. If you already have a great thing going, allow me to refresh what you've learned and/or add to your business vocabulary. All I ask is that you have an open mind and heart to receive this information that I believe will be beneficial to you as an Artist now and in the future.

There are Artists all over the globe that are pursuing music full-time but there is only ONE you! Let me be the first to say embrace your uniqueness and if you would allow me, I would love to assist you in going as far as you possibly can. I believe that this information is vital in growing effective Artist-Producer relationships. This book isn't a verbatim manual to the exact ins and outs of Artist-Producer interactions, but it is based on my 19-years of experience having those interactions with Artists across multiple genres. Let me begin by saying "Congratulations!" You've decided to pursue a career as a musical artist, so let's begin.

"The wise musicians are those who play what they can master."
- Duke Ellington

"We don't know where our first impressions come from or precisely what they mean, so we don't always appreciate their fragility."
-Malcolm Gladwell

no. 1 First Impressions

YOUR SOCIAL MEDIA PRESENTATION

WHAT DOES YOUR SOCIAL MEDIA PRESENTATION SAY ABOUT you? In the current age, social media rules everything. Not in a literal sense, but definitely in a practical one. Social media equates to impact on the culture, impact on the individuals' lives, and guides large groups into the "next new thing." Many of today's stars are found via the internet because executives don't have to leave their homes to surf the web and discover new talent. Social media has also become a visual representation of what you, the Artist, is doing or perhaps what you'd want people to believe you're doing. Which brings me to the question, does your social media page show that you are a musical artist? If not does it show your desire to become one? Any record executive or in this case a

Music Producer should be able to go to any of your social media pages and clearly see that you are pursuing a music career. There are many music moguls that have pages filled with day to day life, vacations, new purchases and other things. Let's be clear, they have already arrived. Artists of that caliber have already developed a grassroots fan base and use their social media to promote new projects and interact with their fans. My aim is to help you build your catalog with great music and have fans all over the world.

Does your social media page reveal the career you're pursuing?

A Producer will know how serious to take you based on your visual representation. Number of followers is something that varies with Indie Artists, however, what should be visible is a clear indication of the career you are trying to pursue. If a Producer looks on your page and sees something other than the representation of your artistry, they may not take you as serious and give you the run-around. If your page is full of pictures flashing money and wearing expensive belts and shoes, a Producer may charge you a standard rate. I am not at all saying that having money in your pocket will mean you will get overcharged, but it doesn't give you much room for negotiation.

For the record the quickest way to misrepresent yourself to a Producer is to have a page with the appearance that you have it all together, but no budget. At the end of the day be sure that your social media presentation falls in line with who you are realistically and what you are trying to accomplish. Be in the present yet present yourself in the best way visually.

Content is a major factor, but all content isn't good content. As an Artist, you should have a visual and audio representation of being an Artist. Let's be honest about one thing, professional visuals cost money. Having a great photographer with an eye and great editing abilities can be very beneficial. However, as an up and coming Artist money is a giant factor so choose wisely. Don't let finances be a stumbling block to your visual effectiveness. Most people have smartphones which have pretty decent cameras. The key point here is to deliver a polished and professional visual experience for your fans. Posting musical content is also a great way to draw attention to yourself in a positive way. These days, new Artists are being discovered based on social media followings which usually happens due to them going viral. A good way to assist that is to post content that goes along with current events, singing covers and doing things to make yourself stand out.

INITIAL GREETINGS

Your first encounter with a Music Producer should be as professional as possible. I say "as possible" because there's no guarantee that your first interaction will be planned out. Be sure not to give the impression that your eagerness to work with them is more important than your respect for them and yourself both as business professionals.

The music industry has many instances where first encounters are made in very intimate or relaxed environments. It's important to be aware of the environment because that can help you gauge the Producer's mood. They may not be in a mood to talk business, or perhaps they may be under an influence that would cause them to not be able to have a productive business interaction at that particular time. Some instances only allow a brief meeting with an exchange of information, and some instances allow for a much longer conversation allowing details. No matter the circumstance, always present yourself in the most respectable way so that you as an aspiring music professional can be taken seriously.

In the event your initial encounter with a Music Producer is done via the internet (social media or email), your delivery and content of your message should be clear and direct. Greet them in a professional way and try not to make your initial pitch to them consist of words that would make you come across as if you know them personally. Here's an example of what your email could possibly say:

Hello [Producer(s) Name],

I'm [Your Name] and I'm a rapper/singer interested in working with you on new music. I have a few songs I have written, and I would love to work with a Producer of your caliber. I understand you are busy making great music, so I am emailing to introduce myself. Please direct me to the best way I can enlist your services whether through website or management. I look forward to hearing back from you and hope to work with you in the near future.

Sincerely,
[Your Name]
[Links to your social media, music, website]

Producers take offense to Artists reaching out to them and not taking them seriously or respecting their craft. This does not mean try to talk as if you know everything. This could come across as being overconfident, try and find a healthy balance. After initial communication, give the Producer a few days to respond. Try not to bombard their inbox with additional messages. If you do not receive correspondence from them after a week or so, try circling back in the future.

One of the best things you can do as an Artist to develop a healthy relationship with a new Producer is taking detailed notes of conversations. Even if they aren't a new Producer to you, it's a good practice to keep notes and paper trails for all correspondence. There are a few reasons why this is very important:

1. Information does not have to be repeated.
2. Prices that are quoted may have changed since your initial interaction and it will be best to have a record of quoted arrangements.
3. It keeps all parties involved on the same page.
4. Being able to recall information will remind the Producer about your initial conversation.
5. It shows professionalism and ensures that you are taken seriously.

I have had so many interactions where I was the only one keeping records of conversations between myself and the Artist. It gets frustrating when I have to remind the Artist about what we had previously discussed and quoted. In my mind, I feel that my time has been taken for granted and that they truly aren't serious about their career or the things initially discussed. Although I keep notes of Artists conversations and correspondence, every Producer may not do this. That doesn't mean that they don't care, they may be very busy and may not have time to write down notes from every single Artist they come in contact with. I assure you that if you are someone that has an established relationship with them, it won't be an issue for them to keep track of this sort of information. My goal is to get you to the point of fostering healthy relationships with these individuals.

Be prepared to present your abilities on demand leaving your shyness at the door.

Lastly, leave your shyness at the door. Expect to present some form of your abilities if asked to. I have been in many encounters where an Artist presents themselves to me and wants to work together. I would ask them to let me hear them sing and all of a sudden there is some unforeseen reason why they can't at that particular time. They aren't warmed up, or they need a beat to rap on, or the worst response which is "I don't know what to sing." For music professionals, it is a huge red flag for an Artist to want an opportunity and not be prepared. If you can tell someone that you are a new Artist they should invest in, then you should be ready to give them a reason to. Trust me when I say that if you are able to blow the Producer away during an initial encounter you can skyrocket yourself to the top of their priority list. I have been out randomly and heard someone singing or freestyling and they initially catch my attention. It's often that I'd approach them after they finish simply because I am always looking for the next "Big Thing." A great way to avoid initial embarrassment or time wasted is with preparation. You never know when you may run into someone who can launch your career's next level.

"You can't knock on opportunity's door and not be ready." - Bruno Mars

no. 2 Have a Budget

DO YOUR RESEARCH

WHEN YOU ARE LOOKING TO START ANY SORT OF PROJECT IT IS an absolute must that you have a budget set in place. Your budget can consist of many things, but the key is to put the music first! Many Artists care so much about how they look in their video or their single artwork that they cut corners on their music. This is a horrible mistake. If you want to be taken seriously and known as a true Artist take heed to this information. The Artists that care more about their appearance than their product will only be known for their appearance and not be taken seriously or respected as a true lyricist or singer. My goal with you is that you offer a complete package and leave your mark with every consumer that comes in contact with your work. For example, if your song is on someone's playlist, the individual will never know what you look like if your music doesn't catch their attention. I remember the days of CD's when Artists would be at the mall or shopping plazas passing out their mixtapes. They didn't have the luxury of presenting incredible artwork. I assure you that when people drove out of that parking lot or left the mall and played the Artist's CD, there was a chance it was thrown out the window because of the music itself. Sure, an Artist can gain followers based on appearance, but when they want to truly capture the ears of listeners, they will ensure their music is of professional quality.

Producers spend time and money showcasing their product and their prices. They build websites, start beat stores, pay for marketing apps and companies to promote their work to the masses. As an Artist, you should look up this information and approach them already knowing their prices and expectations. Please don't make the common mistake of feeling that you are too good to pay a specific fee because it can insult them. It could feel belittling or that they aren't good enough to work with you. You'd be better off not contacting them at all if this is the case. Keep in mind Producers network with each other and talk regularly, so you don't want your likeness to be brought up in one of those discussions for the wrong reasons. Like me, many Producers are willing to work with different budgets but let them make that choice for themselves. It is an insult to lowball a Producer for their work. Producers charge specific amounts based on several reasons:

1. They have a high demand for their work.
2. They have achieved award-winning status and will provide a Grade A level product.
3. Equipment to make music costs a lot of money.
4. Quality has a price.
5. They have spent years investing time and resources into their knowledge, equipment and abilities and deserve to be compensated as such.

QUALITY OVER QUANTITY

Always remember that having quality music is better than having a lot of music that has poor quality. One of the first parts of your budget should consist of quality music production. Before you can go into a studio and record, you're going to need music to record along to. Make sure that you take into consideration not only the cost to pay for the Producer's work that you're inquiring about, but also studio costs to record your new song. Although necessary, artwork and visuals should be taken into consideration after you have already paid for your music production and engineer work. Try not to make the common mistake of running out of money before you have a finished record in hand. This could possibly mean having to push back a release date. It is undoubtedly better that you have a complete record that is mixed and mastered before contracting photographers and graphic artists (which are very important as well). Here is an example of what an Indie Artist's budget should consist of:

1. Music Production.
2. Cost of Studio Recording.
3. Engineer Costs (Mixing and Mastering).
4. Cost of Photographer and editing.
5. Cost of Graphic Designer for Album or Single cover.
6. Music Distribution Cost.
7. Marketing Costs and Promotion Expenses.

Although some budgets may vary in specifics, these things should all be considered when putting together a budget. Please do not insult anyone whose services are being inquired about by telling them all the other things you have to pay for. It is very unprofessional and looks to them as if you are trying to take short cuts or take advantage of their services. If you cannot afford any of your choices, it's best to find someone that you can afford rather than being known as a cheap individual. Most working professionals are connected. Not only can they refer you to someone that may be suitable for you, but their recommendation will also come with information on how you do business. Don't let your good be evil spoken of regarding how you treat people.

no. 3 Learn the Business & Act Accordingly

FAMILIARIZE YOURSELF WITH MUSIC CONTRACTS

WE LIVE IN A DAY AND AGE WHERE THE INTERNET OFFERS MORE information than ever before. Utilize this resource to familiarize yourself with Production contracts and work agreements. I advise my clients all the time about covering themselves for legal purposes. Set yourself apart by educating yourself on standard practices. Taking good notes initially will often come in handy when it's time to sign contracts as well. You would be able to cross-check information initially given to what is being presented to you. This is vital because signing a Contract or Work Agreement will supersede previous verbal or discussed agreements.

17

Contracts come in many different sizes, and some can look very professional or not; however, knowing what should be on them is very important. You want to ensure that all avenues have been disclosed, ensuring future legal ramifications are not on your end. I've had many Artists come to me and ask my opinion about different aspects of their contracts, which is very beneficial to them. However, I spend time educating them on the basic concepts and what they mean, so they will know what to look for in the future. I also direct them to attorneys I am connected with that can thoroughly explain legal terminology.

It is crucial to have an entertainment lawyer oversee the signing process.

I can promise you one thing, the deeper you get into the industry, the more information you will see in Working Agreements and Contracts. They do become standard and relative at a certain level, but by then, I'd hope you would have an Attorney to look over things for you. Although you need to know common terminology and aspects, it is crucial to have an Entertainment Lawyer oversee this process. Sure, they will cost money, but it is better to cover your tracks on the front end than have a lawsuit on the back end. If something is breached in the

Agreement or Contract, that same attorney will ensure that you are compensated accordingly.

UNDERSTAND THE DIFFERENT MUSIC PRODUCTION RIGHTS

I will go through a few different types of Contracts you will come in contact with and briefly explain what they mean. The term Non-Exclusive beats mean you are not the only person who owns the rights to perform on this particular arrangement. This can be both good and bad; allow me to explain why.

If the arrangement is great and has a good beat and feel to it, chances are other Artists feel the same way. So, they lease the beat from the Producer, which gives them the rights to perform and record the song. Sometimes this means the Artist can do paid performances or non-paid performances. Depending on the Producer, things may be different. Why would this be a good or bad thing? If you are a new Artist trying to build a fan base by releasing as much music as you can, this is a great route because it will allow you access to large amounts of music production. However, you are not the only Artist with this music. If that doesn't bother you, then this is indeed a way to go. I engineer sessions often with Artists recording mixtapes using Non-Exclusive beats, and they make a great song. I also have sold these types of rights to allow Artists access to music for a low price.

Keep in mind on the back-end Producers have to make their money as well, so don't be surprised at the number of people that may have the exact track you do. One thing that will drive a Producer crazy is purchasing this type of condition and expecting a different kind of treatment than what is laid out in their contract. Also, keep in mind that stepping outside of the conditions will lead to legal action.

Exclusive Contracts are more costly than the previously mentioned agreement. In this case, the Artist is given exclusive rights to the music production in a way that no other Artist can have. Reading legal information in these contracts in detail is still very important because all Exclusive Agreements are NOT the same. Some producers give up royalty rights, and some don't. Some allow third-party clauses, and some don't. It is imperative to READ thoroughly and understand every aspect before purchasing. Please do not expect to lowball a Producer in this sort of contract because this type of agreement limits them to marrying their precious body of work to your lyrics. Hence as to why the cost is higher than a Non-Exclusive agreement.

Keep in mind there is much more information to both of these types of Contracts, so I would advise you to seek legal assistance and ask as many questions as possible before committing to any agreement. I am not a lawyer, nor do I use the exact same contracts as other Producers; I am merely giving general information that will help save you time and frustration when shopping for production.

TRACK-OUTS VS. 2-TRACKS

When shopping for production, you will see these terms pop up. If you don't see them, please ask the question before you commit to a purchase, and I will explain the difference and why. 2-Tracks are a mix of all production in a stereo left and right file. Many are in MP3 or Wav form, but regardless of the form they are provided, they are without a doubt a mix done by the Producer themselves. You will notice that they are relatively cheaper than their counterparts. The reason being that you cannot alter the mix itself outside of what is already there. Sure, this limits an engineer to what was provided but in some instances this mix is all that is needed to record with. It also takes less time for the Producer to bounce out a 2-Track or MP3 version of a production rather than a Tracked-Out version. When purchasing this type of production, understand its limitations. The elements of the 2-Track or MP3 cannot be generally altered or panned differently to fill up a final mix with vocals.

Tracked-Out versions of production are another form that gives a file for each track in either mono or stereo form. Regardless, this version gives your engineer the ability to fully provide their best ability to have a full and clean overall mix to your song. When dealing with vocalists needing specific levels and pans in their mix, this is the way to go. Now, understand that this version will cost more than the other version—the reason why is that the engineer has the ability to alter the original production. Not only in panning (sending tracks in different directions) but in placement, duplication, drop-outs and other effects. This version allows you to reach the overall song's fullest capabilities. When purchasing this version, make sure that the engineer you hire can reach your complete vision for your song.

Overall, be prepared to see all four of these terms used in different variations with each other with different price points. My goal is to ensure you are familiar enough to have an effective conversation with your Producer and Engineer and get what you are paying for. Keep in mind that prices will vary depending on who you are working with. Please do not try and alter expectations or talk down the Producer. Understand what is being offered and pay their amount. If you cannot afford it, then shop other options for Producers that better fit your budget. This is why having a budget ahead of time is very important, so that when you come to the point of shopping for production, you know what you're looking for and what you can afford. This will make the Producer very happy, and they will take you very seriously if you are familiar with this information ahead of time.

no. 4 Knowing Your Lane

UNDERSTAND YOUR LIMITATIONS

EVERY ARTIST SHOULD HAVE A PREDEFINED VISION FOR WHO they are and what type of music they want to make. A starting point for this is knowing your limitations. When I come in contact with a new Artist looking for production, I ask them if they are a soprano, alto or tenor. This is a very important question because I have to understand the Artist's boundaries. Every Artist that sings soprano doesn't have a lower register, and every alto cannot sing soprano. Although Artists vary in what they can handle, the important thing is to completely understand your boundaries and how to effectively communicate them to your Producer. If you haven't heard this already, let me be the first to tell you what to expect when you come in contact with a new record executive or producer. The first thing they are going to do is look at you and think about your marketability. The second thing they are going to do is ask you to sing for them. Shyness is not the way to go. We look for confidence in both visual representations and vocal ability. Your personality will show exactly how confident you are, but your vocal capability will immediately give sight of your potential. The best way to be confident is to practice your craft and understand what you truly can and cannot do at the moment. Let's not confuse a boundary for laziness because it is not the same thing. Just because you don't like to be pushed vocally doesn't mean you cannot hit certain notes. Just because you aren't confident in your dancing ability on stage doesn't mean you can't dance. Being an Artist is about being vulnerable. There is no room for laziness or a lousy work ethic. If you want to be the best, you have to embrace being uncomfortable.

SURROUND YOURSELF WITH THE RIGHT PEOPLE

How does surrounding yourself with right people help in fostering a great relationship with a Producer? It's very simple. If you put people in your circle that will tell you the truth, it will save a lot of time, money and frustration. For instance, if you are a singer and aren't a talented *runner,* having people around you who hype you up about doing runs will cause embarrassment. Maybe you are a great singer but do "too much" when singing, having people around you that tell you to calm down will be helpful. When you come in contact with a good Producer, they will tell you the truth if they care. If it is something you've never heard before because the people around you only hype you and don't push you to be better, this creates a problem. Now you'll have friction with the Producer and if they are truly invested into you, it can cause a serious issue if you both aren't on the same page.

Surround yourself with people who will tell you the truth about your abilities.

Studio sessions with your Producer can either go really well or very ineffectively if the people you bring are not a benefit. In the past, I have had sessions with Artists and their "entourage" caused more problems than benefits. It is often the wrong people can be overly opinionated and become a distraction to a productive session. When you are in a session with your Producer, please keep the same energy initiated when you reached out to them to begin working. If the people you bring to your session negatively cause any deviation from the previously mapped out goals between yourself and the Producer, "Leave them at home." Everyone in your session should have the same goal and be on the same page.

Here are a few benefits to having positive people in your session:

1. More brains are better than one.
2. Someone may have an idea that could take your song from mediocre to becoming the next radio hit.
3. The right people can keep you motivated and energized.
4. They help you relax and remain comfortable.
5. In the event the Producer tells you something that's beneficial, they can vouch for that, giving you more confidence in what is being said.

In the end, time is money! So, the idea is to make every session a productive one. Limit your distractions and feed your creativity. The worst thing you can do is blow your budget on sessions that aren't productive.

"I've been imitated so well I've heard people copy my mistakes."
- Jimi Hendrix

no. 5 Musical References

WHAT STYLE OF PRODUCTION DO YOU SEEK?

WHEN I COME IN CONTACT WITH AN ARTIST, I AM GOING TO want to know everything about what their goal is sonically. Please don't be offended by this concept, because all music came from an initial source. Creatives have built their passion for music from a root source. Maybe it was old records your parents used to play. Or perhaps growing up in church made you fall in love with music as a child. No matter where your passion came from, it has developed a hunger in you to make what you've learned and studied into your career. I expect you to put a spin on it and make it your own, but it's important to be able to communicate your influences. Artists often take offense when they do not understand this concept because they want to be seen in their own unique way

27

and don't want to be compared to another Artist. Let me be clear, this is in no way comparing you to a legendary artist or current artist in the way of calling you a copycat. It is simply setting a foundation for the type of feeling you are trying to deliver to your audience.

Initially when I hear an Artist sing or rap, I immediately compare their style to someone. In my mind or verbally, I will state who they remind me of in tone, range, delivery or style. Quite often, they say, "I listened to that Artist growing up." Every musical experience along with life circumstances will come out of your vocal cords. Trust me when I say embrace it! Embracing this concept will only help you effectively communicate what you need from your Producer sonically.

PROVIDE SONG EXAMPLES

A great practice to have is providing specific songs that give the feel you want. It may just be a bass line or drum groove. Perhaps it may be chord progressions that provide a necessary feeling that you need your Producer to deliver. If you can provide specific ideas, it gives the Producer a clear indication of the direction you are looking to go. You have to remember that Producers are very creative individuals. Like painters, they create masterpieces on top of absolutely nothing. They start from scratch, so if you don't provide examples and give them free rein to create something, they will create based on how they feel at that moment. Like myself, many Producers make large amounts of tracks or beats daily. They lay concepts based on something they heard or an idea that randomly popped in their head.

As an Artist, it is essential to establish the vision and direction and then trust your Producer to create what you want to hear on your record sonically. It can be very frustrating when I work with clients and they tell me, "Let me see what you come up with," when they don't mean that. I often come back with a composition that I put time and effort into, and the Artist says they wanted something else. If you let a mad dog off a leash, the dog is going to be a dog. You can't let them off the leash and then get mad if they bite someone. With that being said, initiating a blueprint or landscape for the Producer will allow them to see the skeleton as you've mapped it out. It will also let them know how far and how creative they can go in making your vision come to light!

BE ABLE TO COMMUNICATE SOUNDS

In this day and age, Music Producers have unlimited access to sounds and samples. There are hundreds of millions of sounds to choose from; Producers invest in sound kits, sample stores, live instruments, and other things to expand their sonic capabilities and make themselves competitive. As an Artist, it's beneficial if you know specific sounds you are looking to hear. Some Artists are into live instrumentation, and some are into more synth-driven sounds. You have to be able to say something other than "that horn thingy" when describing a trombone. When you think about it, there are so many different horns and sounds. Some are synth and some are live, but more than just communicating the preference, please learn the instrument. If you want to have an effective conversation with a Producer who has access to 3 million sounds, be specific.

To have an effective conversation with a Producer who has access to millions of sounds, be specific in communicating yours.

A great way to accomplish this other than providing song examples is to learn the names and sounds of different instruments. All Artists and Producers were not band students. Many never picked up an instrument in their lives. So, you can't assume the Producer will know what you are visualizing if you aren't able to give them the instrument's name. Also, take into consideration the change in sounds over time. Meaning, a synth sound used in 1960 may not be the same sound the Producer has access to in 2020. Many producers use hardware, some use software and some use both. Understanding the differences in things will only make it easier to communicate your vision to your Producer, allowing for great chemistry. Great chemistry can lead to a great record that both parties can be proud of.

BPMS AND TIME SIGNATURES

A BPM is regarded when describing a song's tempo because it is the beats per minute. Which means the higher the BPM the faster a song will be. Artists often come up with concepts for a new song but don't know anything about time signatures or song tempo. This is very important in properly explaining to your Producer the style of song you want. However, when time signatures are brought into play, it can change the entire flow of the song. Different genres are known for specific time signatures but it's not a guarantee that a Producer will expect a 4/4-time signature when an idea is given. Especially if the Artist sends a concept and there isn't a metronome. Familiarizing yourself with different time signatures will allow you to explore different ways of presenting your musical ideas and vision.

no. 6 Be Coachable

VOCAL COACHES AND VOCAL PRODUCERS

THE KEY TO VOCAL PREPARATION IS WORKING WITH A VOCAL coach. You truly don't have to go far to find a vocal coach. A best practice is to ask a working Artist if they have anyone they would recommend. Most likely, they have one themselves and could connect you. If that individual is too pricey don't give up hope, they may have someone that can fit your budget. I know a few that offer lessons via FaceTime or Skype. I would take advantage of any option you can get your hands on. Invest in one with the credentials and experience to teach you what you need to know. Learning scales, numbers, pitch practices, vocal exercises and warmups will be extremely beneficial.

One of the first things I ask before a recording session is if the singer warmed up already. It is important and will save a lot of time when recording takes, even if it is simply a demo. One of the worst things you can do is record on a Producer's track with bad vocals. Some may not like the performance and ask you to go back or disassociate themselves from promoting the song if it is released. Keep in mind that it's better to have the Producer present when recording the song. If that is not possible, please make sure you have a vocal arranger or vocal producer available. Many Producers have them on hand for sessions or may refer one if they cannot be present. Your vocal coach and the vocal arranger don't have to be the same person, but it's a plus if they are because they can implement things practiced in your coaching sessions.

During your session, the idea is for everyone to be open-minded. The more push back that is given in any regard, the less efficient and productive the session will be. Remain fluid and expect to get constant feedback. You are not always going to like what is suggested; however, it is most likely that the information is for the music's benefit. It can be frustrating when individuals take criticism personally. Try to stay neutral and open as much as possible so that no one involved checks out. Keeping the temperature in the session good will keep the creative juices moving and, in the end, create a great finished product.

PITCH CORRECTION IS CLUTCH BUT NOT A CRUTCH

Music today is much different than it used to be. We have the ability to edit wave files in a way that Producers and Engineers in past decades could not. Punching in recording tracks and using plugins is a given in just about any recording session. Gone are the days where everything had to be recorded perfectly with all singers, background singers and band included. I completely understand that we are no longer in those times, but it has made many Artists lazy. They know that pitch correction and editing is possible and have done away with good practice and technique.

Plugins nowadays can fix vocals in real-time and are often requested when recording. I use these plugins regularly with Artists, but they are used to fix small pitch issues. Producers know the sound that will come out of pitch correctors, and they may not be too interested in having that particular feeling for the song. Some music currently on the radio for rap music and pop songs have pitch blanket effects and sound great! That doesn't mean it is called for in every song being recorded between the Artist and Producer. Many Engineers will indeed tell you that they will only use them if it's called for, so don't get too comfortable depending on pitch correction. Practicing vocal pitch and song execution will help avoid this. It is not uncommon for the key to be completely changed in the production to better fit the vocalist.

no. 7 Follow Through

CORRECT LISTING

CONGRATULATIONS ON COMPLETING YOUR NEW MUSIC. You should be ready to submit your music for publishing credit, distribution, radio, etc. Now is a good time to review initial splits and arrangements. A big issue comes when this is not done correctly, and correct split agreements are not abided by. When in doubt, double and triple check your contract to make sure not to make a mistake here. Proper spelling is also important. You may know your Producer by their stage name, but confirm what they need to be listed by legally to get what is due to them. Contracts work different ways depending on the individual and front-end agreements but regardless of the appropriate split percentage, listing names correctly and in the right place is essential. It also helps to show proof that this step is complete and in the correct way agreed upon. This gives everyone involved a peace of mind knowing all legalities have been done.

Usually, listing and splits are controlled on a Label level. Good Managers also do this for their clients due its importance being done correctly and avoiding lawsuits. They usually complete all the back-end business, so if you have one that is great! I would advise you to learn how to do it for yourself in the event they cannot, or you know longer work with them. No matter the case, it is best to know what is going on with the business side of things, and a good Manager will undoubtedly teach you these things and keep you in the know. Keep in mind, the individuals that took part in the recording are depending on you and your team to handle business correctly. While on the back end of getting ready to release music, keeping open lines of communication is a good way to build trust between Artist and Producer. Many times, communication lines fade out because the front-end has been paid as well as the song recorded, mixed and mastered. However, it is important to keep everyone in the loop. Showing artwork and cover layouts keep anticipation and comradery alive.

no. 8 Give Credit Where It's Due

I OFTEN SEE POSTS ABOUT NEW MUSIC COMING OUT BY INDIE artists who don't show anything about the people behind the record. A lot of music is promoted on social media, giving whomever is posting the opportunity to tag individuals. Although this is a great tool, remember that new releases are a modern-day calling card for individuals in the record. When you have an opportunity, be sure to acknowledge them. This act not only shows appreciation for them, making the vision a reality but also puts in a good word for those looking for the same services. Again, we are looking to foster relationships and build long-standing trust between working professionals.

Interviews are a great time to give "shout-outs" to the Producer behind your song. No matter how big or small the interview is, it's great to show the teamwork it takes to make a great song. Some Producers use these types of promotions to help their platform and showcase the Artists they work with. Using backstories of how you and the Producer came to work together adds some transparency to your story and brings your audience closer to the inner workings of a great record. Another example of giving credit is when an Artist is receiving an award; we often hear them honor their team, which is great publicity for everyone involved.

"The truth is like the sun. You can shut it out for a time, but it ain't goin' away." - Elvis Presley

no. 9 Every Record is a Partnership

BRANDS ARE INTERTWINED

WHEN A SONG IS MADE, A MARRIAGE IS FORMED BETWEEN the lyrics and the music itself. Legally, it becomes a body of work, and legalities must be established before being separated, just like a marriage. When describing legendary songs, we hear the word "Timeless," which describes the song's inability to become outdated. Whether the music is played without the words or not, people will automatically connect the two and often sing the lyrics without the Artist's vocals being present. I said that because brands are intertwined when working with a Producer. Their image and yours are connected, so you both have to be careful when choosing who to work with. All company is not good company, and although a track may sound incredible, there can be baggage attached to it.

Although music should be about the music, there are politics involved with partnership selection. I don't particularly like getting involved with those types of things and love creating great music. However, I am careful about the people I surround myself with both personally and professionally. You should be too! Longevity is created by making timeless music that can cross decades and barriers. Consumers will hear a song come on the radio and immediately change the station or if streaming, change the song simply because of something the Artist did in their personal life.

YOU'RE ASSOCIATED WITH THE PEOPLE AROUND YOU

I've been involved with situations with Artists where I have seen them miss out on collaboration opportunities due to the people around them. The Music Industry is a popularity contest so keep this in mind. It could be another Artist that you affiliate with or maybe partnered with on a collaboration. It's often assumed that collaborations mean you're affiliated personally with the Artist you're collaborating with. Your entourage can also be responsible for you not being able to book time at your favorite studio. People around an Artist may not always be the right people for them. I'm not telling you not to bring your best friend to the studio with you. However, if people don't know how to act or can't quite seem to not draw attention to themselves, they may not be the best people to bring into professional situations.

"The true beauty of music is that it connects people. It carries a message, and we, the musicians, are the messengers." - Roy Ayers

"Life is what happen when you're making other plans."

- John Lennon

no. 10 Don't Burn Bridges

MUSIC LEAKING

OFTENTIMES, AN ARTIST COMES TO THE STUDIO AND GETS A track from me, we record a demo and the first thing they want to do is play their song for everyone. Although I understand the excitement of letting people know you are busy working on new music, you must be careful. If music is not copywritten, it can easily be stolen. This means although sending your new song to friends and other Artists is a normal practice, please cover your tracks. We live in an age where music can so easily be recorded and released; do not send out music if it is not legally protected. Be careful who you share music with, especially if your release date is set down the road. Your music falling into the wrong hands can, in turn, be leaked to a blog or someone looking to have an inside scoop on new updates. It's safe to say that if it is played for people, make sure it's in a controlled environment where cell phones are not recording audio or video. As a Producer involved with many different Artists, I'd rather an Artist play a song for someone than to send it to them before a release date.

RELEASE DATES

To foster healthy relationships with your Producer, be sure to communicate release dates. Many distribution platforms have different requirements for releasing new music, so it is important to have your music submitted ahead of time rather than last minute.

This will ensure the posted release date is accurate. I have worked on albums in the past where stipulations hadn't been met and release dates had already been posted. Of course, the release dates were pushed back. Luckily the dates set were in house, so no embarrassment was suffered by anyone involved. However, this is not always the case. I have also been involved with projects where stipulations were not met, and release dates were publicly communicated. This of course, turned into an embarrassment for everyone involved.

Learn from the mistakes of others so that you do not suffer the same humiliation. Keep in mind that your listeners will hold on to what you communicate, so even if the date is altered, be sure that you or your team communicates it first. Don't let the release date come and the music not be available. Above all, ensure that everyone involved with the record is in the loop, keeping your relationships full of trust and assuring others confidence in your words.

"One thing I've learned is that I'm not the owner of my talent; I'm the manager of it." - Madonna

 *"Despite everything, no one can dictate who you are to other people."*

- Prince

no. 11 Be the Person You Would Want to Work With

TIME IS MONEY

MUSIC PRODUCTION IS A FULL-TIME CAREER. THAT MEANS when music is being created, the Producer is on the clock. In other words, if they are working with an Artist, it is taking away from time they could be working on another project. The concept of time goes both ways because as an Artist, working on a time crunch is pretty normal. Deadlines have to be made and conditions met. So, don't waste unnecessary time. If there is a schedule, then stick to that schedule. As an Artist, it's important to be prompt and be where you are supposed to be when you are scheduled. Studio overhead costs money, and it's best to use all the time possible to get the most work completed. There should be equal consideration of time for everyone involved. A Producer expects to be paid on time, and an Artist expects to get their money's worth.

CHARACTER COUNTS

Character goes a long way in interactions between Artists and Producers. Having a bad attitude or speaking rudely can cause sessions to end badly. Remember as well that industry professionals talk to each other and you don't want to be "That Artist." I have been in sessions where the mood is off due to the Artist talking to the Producer or Engineer disrespectfully. Everyone involved in the creative process needs to have a good working environment for creativity to flow freely. The bottom line is, do what you say you're going to do when you say you are going to do it.

DO IT BECAUSE YOU LOVE IT

When someone loves something, they do everything in their power to show it. This goes for being an Artist as well. True passion is heard and felt when an Artist sings or raps. A listener hears the pain in an Artist's voice or their joy just the same. They perform from their soul and the room stays still. Attendees may have an emotional experience because they can connect with the Artist during their performance and leave feeling fulfilled. It's easy to relate to lyrics when they are felt and not simply heard.

Becoming a successful Artist is a marathon, not a sprint.

Being an Artist is a marathon not a sprint. The way the world is nowadays, pursuing music has to be more than a get rich scheme. One-hit wonders happen, but the question is what happens after that? You truly have to love making music to be successful. At the end of the day, no song is a guaranteed hit record, and every album doesn't get nominated for an award. Every musical Artist won't achieve a million followers on social media, and every post they make will not gain 20,000 likes. What I am saying is, if you get into the music business do it for the right reason. If it is to be popular, rich, get that girl/guy they want or any other reason than the love of music then this isn't for you.

When Artists pursue music for the wrong reasons, it's easy to get burnt out eventually because there is no deep-down hunger to push you past disappointment on a record that has flopped.

Radio Station DJ's may not be willing to play your record and you may not get as many downloads as an Artist hopes for, so what's left after all of that? The love of music will be an inspiration when everything else fades. Keep this in mind when you decide to step into being an Artist, because everyone involved is invested in you with time, resources and their services. When everyone is truly passionate about their craft, the finished product makes it all worth it.

"Musicians don't retire; they stop when there's no more music in them."
- Louis Armstrong

CONCLUSION

---⟨①⟩---

YOUR LIFE BECOMES A STAGE

THIS BRINGS ME TO A VERY IMPORTANT CONCEPT OF BECOMING a public figure. Although your personal life belongs to you, your fans will want to feel close to you. Meaning, when you are in public, it's possible that someone familiar with you will notice you. They may ask for a picture or record you live and share with their friends. Please be prepared for this; I assure you this behavior is normal. With that being said, understand that anything you do will be examined and scrutinized. The level of notoriety you've achieved will reciprocate a multiplied amount of backlash for certain behaviors. A good practice will be to grasp this idea now before it's too late. I'd rather you be prepared than for you to blow up overnight and not be able to handle the notoriety.

You truly never know who is paying attention to you and what your influence means something to someone. A fan can meet you for the first time and your response to them can have a major impact on their perception of you and other Artists. Let people know what you want them to know and keep everything else inside your household. Once it's released to the public, people will not allow it to go away and you can be attached to that particular action in not only the present but also the future.

I am in no way telling you to live according to another person, but it is good to be mindful of their perception of you. As an Artist, you become a mentor to those aspiring to pursue musical careers and business professionals alike. If you have an opportunity to give back or affect the next generation of creatives, it is important to do so whenever possible. Use your platform to enrich the lives of the people your music effects and be the change you want to see.

I want you to be able to embrace what will come along with an exciting musical career. Although outcomes vary for different individuals, your practices should be similar. Here are a few things to keep your talents progressing:

1. Take care of your body.
2. Take care of your voice.
3. Singers, practice your scales.
4. Lyricist, practice your delivery and fluency.
5. Exercise as often as possible.
6. Practice performing in the mirror (It's important to see

what people see).

7. Have time to yourself.

8. Avoid negative interactions and conversations.

Thank you for reading, and I truly believe that the topics discussed in this book will be beneficial to you both as an individual and an Artist.

 *"No matter what happens in life, be good to people. Being good to people is a wonderful legacy to leave behind." - Taylor Swift*

ACKNOWLEDGEMENTS

I have been blessed to have some amazing people in my life that have been with me as long as I can remember. I have also been blessed to have some amazing influences along the way that took me under their wings and showed me the ropes. I would be lying if I said that everything I have achieved was done on my own.

To my mother, you have supported me every step of the way. No matter how big or small my dreams were, you were always right next to me. Your love and prayers have lifted me and helped me through the lowest times and stayed in the great times as well. I appreciate and love you more than you will ever know.

To my father, although I am your namesake you have encouraged me to be my own man. I appreciate the things you've done for me. Thank You.

To my big sister Rea. I know I am bigger than you now but truthfully, I have always looked up to you and am proud to be your little brother. We have been through life's turmoil together and at times only had each other to depend on. I will forever love and appreciate the woman you are. I love you!

To my God sister Fletina, you have been such a blessing to my life. You always seem to be there in my toughest times. You heard my vision and helped make this possible and I can't thank you enough! I love you!

To the rest of my family and friends, I love you all. Thank you for all the love and support you've always shown me.

I can't forget to mention some of the most amazing musical influences in my life that have helped me throughout my career and still influence me today: Lamar "Marz" Edwards, Arthur "Buddy" Strong, Sixx John, Gorden Campbell, Steve "Swiff D" Thornton, James "Dook" Jones, George "Corvelle" Connedy, Bishop Clifton Edwards Jr, Justin Gilbert, Andre Washington, Anthony Cowan, Tarrence Motley, DaJuan Cowan, David Cowan, Rufus Blaq and Deven Reed.

Special thanks to Dennis and Lonnica Crawford, Bria Brown, Jonathan Liggins, Travis Watkins and Namon Jones Sr.

BIOGRAPHY

Professionally known as "GK Jones," Glenn Kenneth Gilliard II is an American recording artist, songwriter, producer and engineer from Poughkeepsie, NY. GK credits his love for music to his maternal grandfather, David Jones Sr., and having spent his early years playing drums in church. His talents later evolved into multiple instruments including saxophone, piano, and guitar. GK began writing and arranging music at the age of 14 in a garage studio belonging to the late George Connedy Sr. in Palmdale, California. While there, GK began producing for local artists and would soon after receive the opportunity to submit music to major recording artists out of Los Angeles, California. Surrounded by Grammy-award-winning producers and songwriters, GK would soon become an in-house producer gaining the attention of recording executives on a national level.

In 2012, GK gained international attention and award consideration as a solo recording artist following the release of his sophomore album. To expand his brand, GK signed with a new recording label in Atlanta, Georgia, in 2013. He would later launch GK Jones Productions LLC, to service as an independent contractor and Edenic World Studios providing music production, artist development, and mixing/mastering services. Since then, GK has helped launch the careers of new artists with chart-topping singles and award-winning albums. GK has developed a reputable name for himself as a rising star in sound and music production. He aspires to not only inspire, but to help guide young creatives into a successful and memorable career while simultaneously working with major recording artists across multiple genres. GK is truly living his dream—providing professional quality and servicing recording artists worldwide.

Follow on Twitter @gkjonesofficial

www.gkjonesproductions.com

Made in the USA
Middletown, DE
18 October 2020

Are you a new Artist struggling to find the right Producer, yet having a hard time?

Do you have a Producer in mind that you want to work with but don't know where to begin?

11 *things* YOUR PRODUCER WANTS YOU TO KNOW **is your go-to resource.**

There's a gap in the industry between Producers and Artists, and in a world full of creatives, it's easy to get lost in the music industry grind.

GK shares 11 points from the mind and experience of a working Music Producer, directed to help develop strong foundational Artist/Producer relationships. Whether you're an up and coming Artist trying to break in the industry or an Independent Artist, this book is for you.

Glenn Kenneth Gilliard II, professionally known as "GK Jones," is an American recording artist, songwriter, producer and engine from Poughkeepsie, New York. GK gained international attentio as a solo recording artist & later launched GK Jones Production LLC, providing music production, artist development, and mixing mastering services, helping to launch the careers of new artists with chart-topping singles and award-winning albums. GK aspire to not only inspire, but to guide young creatives into successful and memorable careers.

@gkjonesofficial

www.gkjonesproductions.com

ISBN 9780578770413

90000

9 780578 770413

THE GREAT DICKENS FAIR® CHARACTER COLORING BOOK

BY DON CARSON